Elijah and prophets of Baal

Story by Penny Frank

Illustrated by Tony Morris

THE LION
STORY BIBLE

22

TRING · BATAVIA · SYDNEY

Т he Bible tells us
how God chose the nation of Israel to
be his special people. He made them a
promise that he would always love
and care for them. But they must
obey him.

Elijah was a prophet, someone who
told the Israelites what God wanted
them to hear. You can find this story
about Elijah in your own Bible, in the
first book of Kings, chapter 18.

Copyright © 1987 Lion Publishing

Published by
Lion Publishing plc
Icknield Way, Tring, Herts, England
ISBN 0 85648 747 3

Lion Publishing Corporation
1705 Hubbard Avenue, Batavia,
Illinois 60510, USA
ISBN 0 85648 747 3

Albatross Books Pty Ltd
PO Box 320, Sutherland, NSW 2232, Australia
ISBN 0 86760 531 6

First edition 1987

Printed and bound in Belgium

**British Library Cataloguing in
Publication Data**

Frank, Penny
Elijah and the prophets of Baal.—(The
Lion Story Bible; 22)
1. Elijah—Juvenile literature
I. Title   II. Morris, Tony, 1938 Aug 2 –
222'.530924   BS580.E4
ISBN 0-85648-747-3

**Library of Congress Cataloging-in-
Publication Data**

Frank, Penny.
Elijah and the prophets of Baal.
(The Lion Story Bible; 22)
1. Elijah, the Prophet—Juvenile
literature. 2. Prophets—Palestine—
Biography—Juvenile literature. 3. Bible
stories, English—O.T. Kings, 1st.
[1. Elijah, the Prophet. 2. Bible stories—
O.T.] I. Morris, Tony, ill. II. Title.
III. Series: Frank, Penny. Lion Story
Bible; 22.
BS580.D4F68 1987   222'.5309505
86-15323
ISBN 0-85648-747-3

There had been no rain in Israel for two
years. And it was all King Ahab's fault.

God had sent the prophet Elijah to tell
the king, 'God is angry because you
have disobeyed him and you worship
false gods. When you start to obey him,
he will send rain.'

King Ahab had taken no notice.
    Now God told Elijah he must go to see the king again.

Elijah walked through the land of Israel. Everywhere was brown and dry. The animals in the fields were thin, because there was no grass. The people he passed looked tired and thin, too. There were no plants on their farms, so they had nothing to eat.

When the people saw Elijah coming, they said, 'You must be very brave. The king is angry. He has been looking for you everywhere.'

When King Ahab saw Elijah coming, he shouted: 'Here comes the trouble-maker!'

Elijah said, 'I'm not the trouble-maker. You are. If you had obeyed God none of this would have happened.'

'You know that you must worship God,' Elijah said. 'Your Baal is a false god. He has no power. Tell the prophets of Baal and the people to meet me on Mount Carmel, and then we shall see which is the real God.'

So King Ahab told the prophets of Baal and all the Israelites to go to Mount Carmel.

Elijah said, 'Let us both offer a bull as a sacrifice. Then you pray to Baal; I shall pray to God. The God who sends fire is the true God.'

When they all reached the top of the
mountain, the prophets of Baal built an
altar of stones.

They put their sacrifice on the altar
but they did not light the fire.

Then Elijah stood up and shouted, so that all the people could hear him.

'It's time you made up your minds. There can only be one living God. Stop trying to serve both Baal and the God of Israel.

'Let us see which God is powerful enough to send fire. Then we will know which is the living God who answers prayer, Baal or the God of Israel.'

13

Elijah told the prophets of Baal to have their turn first. They prayed and shouted to Baal for most of the day.

They clapped their hands and danced around the altar, but no fire came.

15

Elijah started to tease them.

'Baal must be asleep,' he said. 'Shout louder and wake him up. Then perhaps he'll send you fire.'

They started to scream to Baal. They danced faster and faster. But still no fire came.

Now it was Elijah's turn.

He called all the Israelites to come closer, so that they could see what was happening. He piled up stones to make an altar and put his sacrifice on it.

He dug a trench all around the altar.

Then he poured water all over the altar, until everything was soaking wet. The water ran down and filled the trench.

19

Then Elijah stood in front of the altar. He prayed so that everyone could hear him.

'Lord God, please prove to your people that you are the God of Israel. I want them to know that you are the only living God.'

Suddenly there was fire on Elijah's altar. It blazed hot and red, and the smoke swirled into the air. It burned up everything. It even made the water boil away.

The people shouted: 'The God of Israel is the God who hears us. We will serve the living God.'

'You can go home now,' Elijah told the king. 'I can hear the rain coming.'

Away across the sea was a small, dark cloud. It came quickly. Soon the sky darkened and big drops of rain began to fall. God's people had come back to him. The grass would grow again. The thirsty days were over.

The Lion Story Bible is made up of 52 individual stories for young readers, building up an understanding of the Bible as one story — God's story — a story for all time and all people.

The Old Testament section (numbers 1–30) tells the story of a great nation — God's chosen people, the Israelites — and God's love and care for them through good times and bad. The stories are about people who knew and trusted God. From this nation came one special person, Jesus Christ, sent by God to save all people everywhere.

The story of *Elijah and the prophets of Baal* comes from the Old Testament: 1 Kings, chapter 18. Number 21: *Elijah asks for bread* tells how God especially looked after his prophet during the terrible drought. Ahab, who ruled the ten clans in the northern kingdom of Israel, was leading his people astray. His wicked wife, Jezebel, had brought in foreign gods. It seemed as if no one listened to God any more.

So God sent his special messenger, Elijah, with a challenge. Let the people see who was the true God — and then let them choose. When they saw the power of the living God in action, his people returned to him.

The next story in this series, number 23: *Naaman's dreadful secret*, tells how God healed a general from the enemy army of Syria.